Don't Forget!

Harvest Festival

Monica Hughes

Heinemann
LIBRARY

www.heinemann.co.uk/library
Visit our website to find out more information about **Heinemann Library** books.

To order:
 Phone 44 (0) 1865 888066
 Send a fax to 44 (0) 1865 314091
 Visit the Heinemann Bookshop at www.heinemann.co.uk/library to browse our catalogue and order online.

First published in Great Britain by Heinemann Library, Halley Court, Jordan Hill, Oxford OX2 8EJ, a division of Reed Educational and Professional Publishing Ltd. Heinemann is a registered trademark of Reed Educational and Professional Publishing Ltd.

OXFORD MELBOURNE AUCKLAND JOHANNESBURG BLANTYRE
GABORONE IBADAN PORTSMOUTH NH (USA) CHICAGO

Designed by Joanna Sapwell and StoryBooks
Originated by Ambassador Litho Ltd
Printed in China by Wing King Tong

ISBN 0 431 15405 8 (hardback)   ISBN 0 431 15412 0 (paperback)
06 05 04 03   07 06 05 04 03
10 9 8 7 6 5 4 3 2   10 9 8 7 6 5 4 3 2 1

British Library Cataloguing in Publication Data
Hughes, Monica
        Harvest Festival. – (Don't Forget)
        1. Harvest festivals – Juvenile literature
        I.Title
        394 . 2'64

Acknowledgements
The Publishers would like to thank the following for permission to reproduce photographs: Art Directors/Trip p. 24; Bridgeman Art Library pp. 7, 9, 26; Circa Photo Library p. 5; Collections/Brian Shuel pp. 12, 19, 22; Collections/Roger Scruton p. 16; Corbis pp. 6, 11, 17, 21, 25; Corbis/Charles Lenars p. 29; Corbis/Eye Ubiquitous/Paul Hutley p. 4; Corbis/James Ravilious p. 10; Corbis/Michael Yamashita p. 28; Freephoto.Com Library p. 13; Getty Images/Imagebank p. 8; Getty Images/Stone p. 27; Mary Evans Picture Library p. 15; Pictures of Britain p. 14; Trevor Clifford pp. 18, 20, 23.

Cover photograph reproduced with permission of Trevor Clifford.

Our thanks to Stuart Copeman for his assistance in the preparation of this book.

Every effort has been made to contact copyright holders of any material reproduced in this book. Any omissions will be rectified in subsequent printings if notice is given to the Publishers.

Contents

Words printed in bold letters, **like this**, are explained in the Glossary.

What is harvest festival?

In Britain harvest festival is a thanksgiving celebration that takes place in the autumn, usually in September or early October. It is a time when people can show thanks for their food by giving gifts of fruit, vegetables and flowers, which are put on **display** at the festival.

A harvest celebration gives people the opportunity to collect food they have grown and share it with others. There is a tradition in Britain of decorating churches with home-grown fruit and vegetables. Many farming **communities** will celebrate when the **crops** have all been harvested safely.

Harvesting sugar beet

Sukkot

Jewish people celebrate the harvest in the autumn with Sukkot, the Feast of Tabernacles. It is traditional for them to build Sukkot, or shelters with only three sides. These are a reminder to Jewish people of the time their **ancestors** spent wandering without a proper home. The shelters are decorated with plants and flowers to represent the harvest.

Today, much of our food is produced far away from where we live. So at a harvest festival there are also likely to be tins and packages of food from around the world. The celebration is an opportunity to think about all the people involved in the packaging and transporting of food. At the end of the festival the food is packed into baskets and given to **charities**.

A family in their Sukkah

5

The first harvest festivals

Celebrations of the harvest go back thousands of years. A good harvest meant there would be plenty of food, but a bad harvest might mean many would **starve**. People believed that there were gods and goddesses who were responsible for the harvest. After a good harvest people wanted to thank them and so had a special celebration. If the harvest was not good and failed, people believed the gods and goddesses were angry with them. Even so, they would still hold a harvest festival to ask the gods and goddesses to help them in the following year.

A picture of Demeter on a very old Greek vase

A two hundred-year-old painting of Ceres

The Greek goddess of the harvest was Demeter. A Greek **myth** tells the story of her daughter, Persephone. The king of the **underworld** kidnapped Persephone. This made her mother, Demeter, so angry that she made the **crops** fail and there was a terrible **famine**. Eventually Persephone was allowed back to Earth, but for three months each year she had to return to the underworld. The three months **correspond** with the winter months, when nothing will grow.

Ceres

The Roman goddess of farming was called Ceres. Ceres' name gives us the word 'cereal'. Barley, wheat, oats, maize, rye and rice are all kinds of cereal. Sometimes the word 'corn' is used to describe the main cereal crop of a country or area.

What is Lammas?

In ancient Britain the **Celts** held a celebration on 1 August to mark the end of the summer. This was the time of the corn harvest. They also had 'Mabon' around 21 September to celebrate the harvest of fruit. The full moon that happened at this time was called the harvest moon. Mabon was the autumn **equinox**, when the days started being shorter than the nights. It marked the beginning of winter.

Later, in the Middle Ages, the Church named 1 August 'Lammas day'. It became a celebration of the beginning of the harvest. The first corn to be harvested was made into little round loaves of bread. These loaves were then taken to church to be blessed. Lammas means 'loaf-mass'. Special fairs were also held at Lammas, with processions, dancing and decorated stalls.

A wheat field ready to be harvested

A painting of a country fair from a hundred years ago

Lammas was an important day, especially in villages where there was Lammas land. This was land that could be used by anyone for **grazing** animals. It could not be used before 1 August, by which time the grass that was grown on it would have been cut and dried to use as hay.

The first day in August is still known as Lammas day and is celebrated in parts of Scotland.

Did you know?

A special Lammas loaf can be baked in a clay flowerpot. Long ago, bread was baked in **earthenware** pots rather than the tins that are used today. A new, clean clay flowerpot that has been well greased will make an unusual shaped loaf.

Bringing in the harvest

In the past, people living in Britain depended on their **crops** for food. If the crops suffered from disease and did not grow properly there was danger of **starvation**. A good harvest depended on the right amount of sun and rain at the correct time. If there was too little rain when the crops were growing, or too much rain when the crops were cut, the harvest could be poor.

All the crops used to be harvested by hand. **Scythes** and **sickles** were used to cut down the stalks. The stalks were then tied by hand into bundles called sheaves. The sheaves were shaped into **stooks** and then left to dry. When they were dry, the stooks were stacked and

Farmers harvesting wheat by hand

A hay wagon in 1934

brought in from the fields. Later the stacks were pulled apart and the grain separated out by **threshing**.

The person in charge of the harvest was called 'Lord of the Harvest'. It was his job to tell each worker what he or she had to do. When the harvest was completed, the Lord of the Harvest would drive the last wagon home.

Did you know?

When crops were cut by hand it took at least a day to clear half a **hectare**. Machines made harvesting much faster. An early combine-harvester could often clear 12 hectares in a day. The machine combined reaping (cutting the crop) with threshing (separating the grain).

 # What is celebrated at harvest-home?

The Harvest-Home painted in 1813

In the past, there was always a great celebration at
the end of harvest time. People living in the country
depended on the harvest for their future. Before
machines were used, all the work was done by hand.
Everyone was involved – men, women and children.
Horses pulled loaded wagons, the last of which was
often beautifully decorated. It carried the Lord of the
Harvest and his wife or girlfriend who was known
as the 'Queen of the Harvest'.

When all the work was completed everyone sat down together for the harvest-home feast. This was very unusual, as the workers didn't usually mix with their master.

There was roast beef and goose to eat, followed by plum pudding. Lots of beer and cider were drunk and the oldest harvester proposed a **toast** to the farmer.

Wild games were played with lots of singing and dancing.

A harvest display of fruit and vegetables

Harvest games

A popular harvest-home game from Sussex was called 'Turn the Cup Over'. A horn was filled with beer. The horn was then carefully placed on the top of a top hat. The aim of the game was to try and lift the top hat, holding the brim with both hands, and drink the beer from the horn.

13

What are corn dollies?

In the past, people in Britain believed that a corn goddess lived in the fields. She was worshipped as the protector of the **crop**. As the crop was cut it was thought that the corn goddess was left hiding in the last few stalks left standing. As the last stalks were cut, the workers hid their faces so that they didn't offend the corn goddess.

The last stalks were made into corn dollies to keep the corn goddess alive. Corn dollies were made in many different shapes including a fan, a spiral, a horseshoe and a **crescent** moon.

A woman making traditional English corn dollies

Corn dollies were kept in a safe place until it was time to prepare for the next harvest. When the fields were first **ploughed** in January, many corn dollies were ploughed into the ground. Other corn dollies were burnt – and the ashes scattered in the fields. Corn dollies were never just thrown away, because this would insult the corn goddess.

Corn dolly in the shape of a woman

Hip, hip, hooray

The last stalks to be cut were called the 'nek' or 'mare' in parts of England, the 'hag' in Wales, the 'kirn' in Scotland and the 'carley' in Ireland. When they had been cut they were held up high in the air and a special greeting was shouted; known as the 'harvest shout' – hip, hip, hooray.

What is the harvest of the sea?

Corn, vegetables and fruit could be called the harvest of the land. If you lived by the sea or a port, you could see a different type of harvest – the harvest of the sea. Once a year, the fishing boats are blessed and this is usually followed by a harvest festival. The houses of the fishing **fleet** are sometimes decorated with flags and flowers. The churches are usually decorated with fishing nets and other fishing equipment.

A service to celebrate the harvest of the sea is held at St Mary-at-Hill near London's old Billingsgate Fish Market on the first Sunday in October. Fish are displayed

Blessing the fishing boats in Whitby, North Yorkshire

in the church porch and sometimes there are as many as 39 different kinds there.

Fishing takes place in Britain mainly between May and October, so most harvest celebrations are held in October. In northern Scotland, deep-sea fishing ends on 1 August, so harvest festivals are held at Lammas. Fishing finishes much later in the Isle of Man, so their celebration, a boat supper, is held on 20 December.

The harvest of the sea

Oyster calendar

Oysters are a kind of shellfish. They are now a luxury food but were once so cheap that they were the main food of people living near the Thames. Oysters are in season when there is an R in the month, so they can be enjoyed in September, October, November, December, January, February, March and April.

17

 # The fruit and vegetable harvest

Fruit and vegetable harvest

Fruit and vegetables have a special place in any harvest display. They are ready for harvesting at different times of the year. In Britain, strawberries are the first fruit to **ripen** and the harvest starts in June. Long ago, before canned fruit, frozen foods and imported fruit and vegetables, strawberries could only be eaten when they were in season.

The potato is the last vegetable **crop** to be harvested, and this takes place in the autumn.

Pearly Kings
and Queens

All summer long different fruits and vegetables are
grown and harvested. There are summer fruits like
raspberries, loganberries, redcurrants and blackcurrants,
also juicy cherries and long stems of rhubarb. Colourful
vegetables like yellow sweetcorn, purple aubergines,
orange carrots, red beetroots, green courgettes, spinach
and broad beans, and plump green and white marrows.

Pearly harvest

A special and colourful harvest festival of fruit
and vegetables takes place on the first Sunday
in October. It is organized by the market
traders of London. A service is held at St Martin's-
in-the-Fields Church in Trafalgar Square. There is a
grand parade of **Pearly Kings and Queens**, who
raise money for **charity**.

19

What is apple day?

In some parts of the British Isles there is a special day in October to celebrate just one type of fruit – the apple. Have you ever been to an apple day event or celebration? It is an opportunity to celebrate British and Irish apple **orchards** and the fruit grown in them.

There are **displays** of apples with perhaps as many as 400 different varieties on view. It may be possible to taste many of these different apples. There may also be cookery demonstrations showing how apples can be used in both sweet and savoury dishes. Apples are **pressed** so that the apple juice can be tasted. Cider made from apples is also available.

Variety of food and drink to enjoy on apple day

Apple harvest

Games like apple-bobbing are played. Apples are placed in a large tub of water and you have to eat them without touching them with your hands. There are also competitions including one to find who can make the longest **continuous** piece of peel from one apple. One year the record was a piece over 3 metres (11 feet) long!

Wildlife

The large number of trees in an apple orchard also encourages wildlife. Badgers, deer, rabbits, shrews and voles enjoy the safety of an orchard. Many different birds also visit them. Apple orchards are also home to a variety of wild flowers. Grass snakes, slow worms, toads and frogs may be found in the long grass.

Harvest festivals in churches

The first harvest festivals to take place in churches were in the 1840s. They took the form of a **service** in church followed by a tea party. Within ten years, the **custom** had become well established.

Churches still have harvest festivals today. They are very popular services and take place all over the country in villages, towns and cities.

The church is decorated with flowers, fruits and vegetables given by local people. A local baker might make bread in the shape of a sheaf of corn and this is often the centre of the harvest **display**. A glass of water and a piece of coal are often included in the display, as a reminder of different types of harvest.

Harvest festival at St Mary's Church, Bristol

Fruit and vegetables collected for a harvest festival

Special hymns and prayers are said and afterwards the harvest gifts go to local hospitals, **charities** or needy families.

Harvest hymn

In 1844 Henry Alford wrote this hymn, which is still sung at harvest festivals.

Come ye thankful people, come,
Raise the song of Harvest-home:
All is safely gather'd in,
Ere the winter storms begin;
God our maker doth provide
For our wants to be supplied;
Come to God's own Temple, come;
Raise the song of Harvest-home

Do you have a harvest festival in your school?

A special harvest festival assembly takes place in many schools during the autumn term. Children and their families are asked to give harvest gifts. These often include tinned and packaged food. Many schools help children grow their own vegetables and share them with others. These range from potatoes to beans, to mustard and cress. All the different foods are used to make a harvest **display** that is the centre of the assembly.

Harvest festival assembly in a primary school

A school harvest festival can be made more special by inviting parents and friends of the school to join in. Children can sing special songs, **recite** poems and perform plays as part of the celebrations. Afterwards the harvest gifts are usually given to local **charities**. Perhaps to a shelter for homeless people or a soup kitchen where the homeless can go to get food.

Children in fancy dress for their harvest festival

Would you give up lunch?

At some schools, older children are asked to experience what it would be like to live in an area where the harvest had failed. The children are asked to have only a glass of water and a chunk of bread for their mid-day meal. They then collect the money they would have spent on their normal meal. The money is given to a charity that helps people suffering because of poor harvests or **famine**.

25

What is Thanksgiving?

A modern tapestry called *Landing of the Pilgrim Fathers, 1620*

In the USA, the fourth Thursday in November is a special day to give thanks for all the good things that have happened in the previous year. Americans who live abroad also celebrate Thanksgiving. The celebrations take place in many parts of Britain and Europe.

Thanksgiving remembers the first English **pilgrims** who went to live in America in the 1620s. Many of the **settlers** died during the first winter of hunger and sickness. After their first corn harvest they celebrated with a harvest festival that lasted for three days.

Canadian Thanksgiving

In Canada, Thanksgiving is held on the second Monday in October. It is similar to the American celebration but with different food. Ham and lamb are often eaten instead of turkey. There is also sometimes a pastry pie filled with layers of potatoes, rabbit and perhaps **pheasant** or **partridge**.

They ate turkey, goose and duck as well as smoked eels and clams. Games were played and there was target-shooting with bows and arrows.

Americans now celebrate with a family meal of turkey and cranberry sauce. Followed by special Thanksgiving pies, which are usually made out of pumpkin.

Family enjoying a Thanksgiving meal

Harvest festival around the world

Harvest festival takes place in other countries at different times of the year depending on the seasons. In Europe it takes place between August and October, but in Australia and New Zealand it is between February and March. In Italy and France there are special celebrations in November when the grapes are ready to be picked and made into wine.

The type of **crop** being harvested may also be different. In Australia there is a sheep-**sheering** festival. Farmers celebrate the thick wool that has been grown by their sheep during their winter months.

Harvesting wool in Australia

Traditionally dressed dancers at a French harvest festival

In China a special festival takes place in September, at the time of the full moon. It is to celebrate the rice harvest. Animal shaped lanterns are carried in a procession and lots of different kinds of mooncakes made of rice, are eaten. Children are allowed to stay up late and watch the full moon rise.

African harvest

In parts of Africa, 'Kwanza' is celebrated. Kwanza means 'first fruits of the harvest'. The celebration lasts for seven days between 26 December and 1 January, the time of harvesting in Africa. Gifts are given and it is an opportunity to look back over the past year and think about what has been achieved.

 # Glossary

ancestors relations who lived a long time ago

Celts people who lived in ancient Britain before the Romans

charities (**charity**) organizations that raise money to help people

communities groups of people who live in the same area

continuous going without a break

correspond match or equal

crescent curved shape

crops plants grown for food

custom the usual way of doing things

display to put things on show

earthenware pottery made of baked clay

equinox a day twice a year, when night and day are the same length

famine shortage of food in a country

fleet group of vehicles

grazing animals feeding on grass

hectare area of land of a certain size

myth old story or legend, often about gods or heroes

orchard place where fruit trees grow

partridge bird shot for sport

Pearly Kings and Queens men and women from London who decorate their clothes with pearl buttons and raise money for charity

pheasant long tailed bird, shot for sport

pilgrims people who go on a journey to a holy place

ploughed soil turned over with a plough

pressed crushed or squeezed

recite say something aloud from memory

ripen ready to be picked or eaten

scythe large tool with a curved blade for cutting crops

service religious ceremony

settlers people who go to live in a place

sheering cutting the fleece off sheep

sickle a small tool with a curved blade for cutting crops

starve (**starvation**) die from hunger

stook group of sheaves left standing in a field

threshing beating a crop to separate the grain

toast drink in honour of someone

underworld place in myths and legends where spirits
   of the dead live

Index